Answer Key

Unit 1
The Rajah's Rice

Sentences
page 1

Paragraphs should describe in complete and correct sentences the thing the student knows well.

What are the Four Types of Sentences?
page 2

1. E, exclamation mark
2. Q, question mark
3. C, period
4. S, period
5. S, period
6. Q, question mark
7. S, period
8. C, period
9. E, exclamation mark
10. C, period

Statements and Questions
page 3

1. S, period
2. S, period
3. Q, question mark
4. S, period
5. Q, question mark
6.–9. Statements and questions will vary.

Commands and Exclamations
page 4

1.-5. Commands and exclamations will vary.
6. C, period
7. E, exclamation mark
8. N, question mark
9. E, exclamation mark
10. C, period

Four Types of Sentences
page 5

Paragraphs should describe times students were helpful and use the four types of sentences correctly with correct end punctuation.

A Little Excitement

Complete Subjects and Predicates
page 6

Paragraphs should describe the exciting event in complete sentences and use end punctuation correctly.

What Are Complete Subjects and Predicates?
page 7

Complete subjects are listed first; complete predicates are listed last.

1. My friend Nat and his family; heat their house with a wood stove.
2. Nat and his parents; chop a lot of wood each winter.
3. Several large trees; fall every year in the woods.
4. My sister and I; helped them haul in a large ash tree.
5. This one ash tree; kept Nat's family warm for three weeks!
6.–10. Sentences will vary.

Complete Subjects in Sentences
page 8

1. Families on small farms
2. Many farmers
3. Farming equipment
4. All four seasons
5. Dairy cows
6.–10. Answers will vary.

Complete Predicates in Sentences
page 9

1. perform an important service.
2. have volunteer fire departments.
3. don't live at the firehouse.
4. live in their own homes.
5. gather quickly whenever the fire alarm sounds.
6.–10. Answers will vary.

Fragments
page 10

1, 4, 7 and 9 are sentences. 2, 3, 5, 6, 8, and 10 will vary.

1. S
2. F
3. F
4. S
5. F
6. F
7. S
8. F
9. S
10. F

The Lost Lake

Simple Subjects and Predicates
page 11

Postcards should describe a camping trip as well as use subjects and predicates correctly.

What Are Simple Subjects and Predicates?
page 12

The simple subject is listed first; the simple predicate, last.

1. camping; is
2. It; combines
3. You; carry
4. camping; gives
5. you; get
6. you; will need
7. bike; is
8. kind; will do
9. you; will need
10. Panniers; are
11. They; attach
12. panniers; ride
13. gear; is
14. You; can use
15. you; should wear

Simple Subjects in Sentences
page 13

1. Our fourth-grade class; class
2. These famous mountains; mountains
3. Many lovely lakes; lakes
4. Campers from all over the country; Campers
5. The trails of the Rocky Mountains; trails
6. The campgrounds in the area; campgrounds
7. Rangers in Rocky Mountain National Park; Rangers
8. Campers in the park; Campers
9. Summer storms; storms
10. Unprepared hikers; hikers

Simple Predicates in Sentences
page 14

1. was the first national park in the world; was
2. created the park in 1872; created
3. is certainly Old Faithful; is
4. thrills tourists every year; thrills
5. erupts regularly; erupts
6.–10. Sentences will vary.

Compound Subjects and Compound Predicates
page 15

1. compound subj. Amber, Adam, mother
2. compound pred. bought, packed
3. compound pred. were sitting, talking
4. compound pred. checked, double-checked
5. compound subj. Adam, Amber
6.–10. Sentences will vary.

Sarah, Plain and Tall

Sentence Combining
page 16

Paragraphs should describe the new friend, as well as use compound sentences correctly.

Combining Sentences with Two Predicates
page 17

1. Settlers on the prairie worked hard and went to sleep tired.
2. Prairie soil was very firm and needed a special plow.
3. Farmers raised chickens and grew crops.
4. For pets, settlers kept dogs and raised cats.
5. Cats were good companions and also caught mice.
6. Prairie settlers hunted and fished.
7. Horses pulled the settlers' wagons and dragged the plows.
8. Settlers bought supplies and met friends in town.

Combining Sentences with Two Subjects
page 18

1. The horse and the colt ran over to the barrel.
2. The boy and girl led the horse to the stable.
3. The barn and the chicken coop are made of wood.
4. The horses and other animals need water every day.
5. The horses and sheep eat hay in the winter.
6. Foxes and coyotes would like to get into the chicken coop.
7. Cleaning out the stables and stacking the hay in the loft are big jobs.
8. Hay and straw are cut in the summer.

Sentence Combining: *and/but*
page 19

(sample answers)

1. Nebraska is a prairie state, but Maine is near the ocean.
2. Maine is a part of the United States, and Quebec is a part of Canada.
3. Many people in Maine are sailors, but many in Nebraska are farmers.
4. Maine has many pine trees, but Nebraska has few.
5. The largest city in Maine is Portland, and the largest city in Nebraska is Omaha.
6. Lincoln is the capital of Nebraska, and Augusta is the capital of Maine.
7. Maine's nickname is the Pine Tree State, and Nebraska's is the Cornhusker State.
8. Nebraska is a large state, but Maine is a small state.

Run-ons
page 20

(sample answers)

1. My family lives in Nebraska. My parents are farmers in the western part of the state.
2. I have two brothers and a sister. We help out on the farm. I like living on a farm.
3. We raise hogs on our farm. We have about 500 sows, which are female pigs.
4. We grow corn to feed to our hogs, and we harvest it in the fall.
5. My favorite time is when the piglets are born. They are so cute! I like to pick them up and hear them squeal.

Unit 2
Seal Journey

Nouns
page 21

Students' paragraphs should accurately describe the animal and explain their reasons for liking it, in addition to using nouns correctly.

What Is a Noun?
page 22

1. Seals, babies, ice
2. places, world, seals
3. seals, journeys, autumn
4. author, photographs, babies
5. photographer, helicopter, Canada
6.–10. Sentences will vary.

Common Nouns
page 23

Paragraphs will vary.

Proper Nouns
page 24

Common nouns will vary. Possible answers are given.

1. Jacques Cousteau, explorer
2. *Calypso,* ship
3. Caribbean Sea, ocean
4. John Denver, composer
5. France, country

Nouns should be capitalized or lowercased as follows:

1. people
2. Canada
3. Alaska
4. Inuit
5. Inuit
6. Eskimos
7. Inuits
8. cities
9. towns
10. way
11. life
12. citizens
13. Canada
14. United States
15. governments
16. Canada
17. America
18. Inuit

Titles and Abbreviations
page 25

1. Dr. Melissa A. Parmenter
2. Sept. 21.
3. Bryan St.
4. Centennial Dr.
5. Mr. Harold Edgar
6. August
7. Governor
8. Monday
9. Mister
10. Company

Do Not Disturb

Plural Nouns
page 26

Paragraphs should describe an animal and some amazing things that it does, as well as use plural nouns correctly.

What Is a Plural Noun?
page 27

1. Large grizzly bears wait beside a stream.
2. The bear's cubs roll on the ground.
3. Birds chirp in a tree above the bear.
4. Raccoons drink from the stream.
5. Fluffy white clouds are in the blue sky.
6. Summer breezes rustle the leaves of the trees.
7. Footsteps echo through the forest.
8. Twigs break with a sharp snap.

Plural Nouns with *-s* and *-es*
page 28

1. dishes
2. gases
3. nights
4. rocks
5. churches
6. classes
7. pitches
8. cars
9. splashes
10. foxes

11.–15. Answers will vary.

Plural Nouns with *-ies* and *-eys*
page 29

1. babies
2. journeys
3. C
4. stories
5. cities
6. cross out vallies, write valleys
7. cross out holidaies, write holidays
8. cross out blackberrys, write blackberries
9. cross out toyes, write toys
10. cross out pennys, write pennies

Plural Nouns
page 30

1. Zoos
2. C
3. babies
4. puppies
5. Students
6. C
7. branches
8. donkeys
9. C
10. zoo keepers

Why Frog and Snake Never Play Together

More Plural Nouns
page 31

Paragraphs should imaginatively explain the origins of some natural phenomenon and should use plural nouns correctly.

Nouns That Form Plurals by Changing *-f* or *-fe* to *-ves*
page 32

Plurals should read as follows. Sentences will vary.

1. knives
2. halves
3. lives
4. calves
5. elves
6. thieves
7. shelves
8. wolves
9. loaves

Special Plural Nouns
page 33

Plurals should read as follows. All sentences except 3 and 10 should be rewritten.

1. teeth
2. feet
3. C
4. women
5. feet
6. men
7. mice
8. geese
9. oxen
10. C

Special Singular and Plural Nouns
page 34

Plurals should read as follows. Sentences 1, 2, 4, and 9 should be rewritten.

1. salmon
2. sheep
3. C
4. moose
5. C
6. C
7. C
8. C
9. deer
10. C

More Plural Nouns
page 35

Plurals should read as follows. Sentences will vary.

1. knives
2. men
3. fish
4. women
5. sheep
6. wolves
7. children
8. deer
9. calves
10. mice

A Kettle of Hawks

Possessive Nouns
page 36

Paragraphs should accurately describe a group of animals, as well as use possessive nouns correctly.

What Is a Possessive Noun?
page 37

1. Amanda's
2. bee's
3. beehive's
4. drones'
5. spring's
6. bees'
7. queen's
8. sister's
9. tree's
10. drones'

Forming Singular Possessive Nouns
page 38

1. autumn's
2. sky's
3. wind's
4. current's
5. season's
6. worker's
7. orchard's
8. limb's
9. swarm's
10. air's
11.–15. Answers will vary but should include an appropriate singular possessive noun.

Forming Plural Possessive Nouns
page 39

1. geese's gaggle
2. clams' bed
3. whales' pod
4. ducks' paddle
5. chickens' brood
6. coyotes' band
7. beavers' colony
8. deer's herd
9. lions' pride
10. fish's school

Sentences will vary, but the following possessives should be used.

11. fields'
12. sheep's
13. children's
14. leaves'
15. ponds'

Possessive Nouns
page 40

Cross out these incorrect possessives: *familys, brother, clocks, parents, cats', suns, trees's, brothers, deers, birds's.* Corrected paragraph should look like this:

The woods behind our (family's) house is a very interesting place. My younger (brother's) and my favorite thing to do is to take a walk there early in the morning. As soon as we hear the alarm (clock's) loud buzzing, we leap out of bed. We walk quietly past our (parents') room so we don't wake them up. Buddy the (cat's) puzzled look doesn't bother us! We put on our boots and head out the back door. The (sun's) first rays are starting to warm up the grass. The wind rustles the (trees') leaves. I hold my (brother's) hand when we cross the stream. Sometimes we hear a (deer's) snorting as it runs away. The (birds') singing is so loud you can barely hear anything else!

Unit 3
Mom's Best Friend

Action Verbs
page 41

Paragraphs should accurately describe some sights, sounds, smells, and other experiences of your town, as well as use action verbs correctly.

What Is an Action Verb (1)?
page 42

1. saved
2. walked
3. jumped
4. rescued
5. praised
6. lapped
7. teaches
8. sniffed
9. arrested
10. wiggled
11.–15. Sentences will vary.

What Is an Action Verb (2)?
page 43

(sample answers)

1. They write letters in class.
2. We often stroll around the park.
3. Mark laughed at the joke.
4. The pony galloped around the ring.
5. My dad swims a mile three times a week.
6. Our family eats dinner at six o'clock.
7. I brush my hair every night.
8. Cross the street when the light turns green.
9. The girl scolded her puppy when it ran out in the street.
10. Teach me to play chess, please.

Action Verbs: Fill In the Blanks
page 44

Action verbs will vary but should make sense.

Action Verbs
page 45

goes	vacuums
divide	scrubs
go	washes
do	carries
prepares	cuts

Justin and the Best Biscuits in the World

Present Tense
page 46

Lists should describe the lessons learned and should be phrased in the present tense, with verbs used correctly.

Singular Subjects: Add *-s* or *-es*
page 47

1. mixes
2. checks
3. fries
4. thinks
5. watches
6. buzzes
7. meows
8. washes
9. misses
10. worries

Plural Subjects: Do Not Add *-s* or *-es*
page 48

1. The (horses shake) (their heads) in anger.
2. The (boys smooth) the covers on (their beds).
3. (Opossums carry) (their) babies on (their backs).
4. (Flies buzz) around Grandpa's head.
5. (Cowboys fix) the fence.
6. (Animals splash) in the stream.
7. (Rattlesnakes catch) (mice).
8. The (boys pass) the biscuits to (their) grandfather.
9. The (cooks stew) the raisins.
10. The ranch (hands hurry) to finish the job.

Singular and Plural Subjects
page 49

Sentences will vary, but the verb endings should be underlined as follows.

1. toss, toss<u>es</u>
2. switch, switch<u>es</u>
3. bury, bur<u>ies</u>
4. eat, eat<u>s</u>
5. poke, poke<u>s</u>

Present Tense
page 50

Singular verbs (to be underlined) and their subjects:
works; grandfather
rides; He
inspects; Grandpa
marks; he
makes; grandfather
fries; He
work up; I
gets; brother
take; I
gives; brother
comes; turn
disappears; pork
wash; I
dries; Grandpa
puts; brother

Plural verbs (to be circled) and their subjects:
visit; brother and I
help; We
fix; Men
taste; biscuits
need; horses
drink; they
eat; we
go; biscuits
clean up; we
ride; we

Felita

Past Tense
page 51

Paragraphs should describe the misunderstanding and its resolution, as well as use past-tense verbs correctly.

Verbs in the Past: Add *-ed*
page 52

1. presented	6. hunted
2. landed	7. elected
3. sailed	8. loved
4. helped	9. asked
5. planted	10. wanted

Verbs in the Past: Change *y* to *i* and Add *-ed*
page 53

1. worried
2. tried
3. carried
4. buried
5. hurried
6. Aunt Jane (replied) quickly when I (sent) her a letter.
7. If my sister (married) the gym teacher, he (would) be my brother-in law!
8. The suspect (denied) that she committed the crime.
9. Her brother (studied) very hard.
10. A horse (whinnied) when I (went) into the stable.

Verbs in the Past: Double the Final Consonant and Add *-ed*
page 54

Paragraphs should competently describe a class project and use at least five of the listed verbs. All form the past tense by doubling the final consonant and adding *-ed*.

Past Tense
page 55

Answers will vary but should follow the rule for past-tense verbs at the top of each column.

Teammates

Have, Be, Do
page 56

Paragraphs should describe a friend and his or her differences, as well as use forms of the three verbs correctly.

Using *Have*
page 57

1. has	6. have
2. have	7. had
3. had	8. have
4. had	9. had
5. has	10. has

Using *Be*
page 58

1. is	6. is
2. was	7. are
3. were	8. was
4. are	9. were
5. was	10. are

Using *Do*
page 59

1. do
2. did
3. did
4. do
5. Does
6.–10. Sentences should describe whom the student admires and why, as well as use the forms of *do* correctly.

Have, Be, Do
page 60

Sentences should be on the subject of a favorite sport or activity and use the verb form correctly.

Unit 4
City Green

Main and Helping Verbs
page 61

Paragraphs should describe the project, as well as use main and helping verbs correctly.

What Is a Main Verb?
page 62

1. planning	6. watching
2. helping	7. worked
3. torn	8. helped
4. sat	9. plant
5. carried	10. hoping

What Is a Helping Verb?
page 63

1. has, <u>lived</u>	6. will, <u>play</u>
2. have, <u>joined</u>	7. are, <u>practicing</u>
3. are, <u>helping</u>	8. was, <u>working</u>
4. am, <u>supervising</u>	9. had, <u>decided</u>
5. is, <u>helping</u>	10. will, <u>help</u>

Practice with Main and Helping Verbs
page 64

Verbs may vary slightly.

1. H, was	6. M, grown
2. M, planted	7. M, trying
3. M, planting	8. H, were
4. H, have	9. H, Will
5. H, were	10. M, hoping

Main and Helping Verbs
page 65

Sentences will vary but should include a form of the words listed.

Whales

Linking Verbs
page 66

Paragraphs should adequately describe the whale-watching tour, as well as use linking verbs correctly.

Be in the Present
page 67

1. Whales	6. is
2. is	7. is
3. is	8. are
4. ocean	9. visitors
5. is	10. am

Be in the Past
page 68

1. was	4. was
2. were	5. were
3. was	

Completed sentences will vary.

6. Shannon and Maria were
7. A narwhal was
8. You were
9. The whale-watching trip was
10. Several humpback whales were

Be in the Future
page 69

1. The ocean (will be) very calm tonight.
2. I (will be) on the main deck of the boat.
3. My sister and I (will be) the first to sign up for this trip.
4. We (will be) members of the Nature Club at school.
5. The leader of the trip (will be) Ms. Jackson.
6. Many Nature Club members (will be) interested in whale-watching.
7. I (will be) vice president of the club (next) year.
8. My sister (will be) club president (next) year.
9. My favorite whale (will be) the gray whale.
10. Ms. Jackson and I (will be) hopeful that we (will) see one on this trip.

Linking Verbs
page 70

1. will be, <u>Kristen</u>
2. were, <u>members</u>
3. am, <u>I</u>
4. is, <u>film</u>
5. are *or* will be, <u>William and Martin</u>
6. was, <u>Sarah</u>
7. are, <u>Whales</u>
8. will be, <u>Whales</u>
9. is, <u>meeting</u>
10. were, <u>Sarah and I</u>

Just a Dream

Irregular Verbs
page 71

Paragraphs should describe how the student helped the environment and should use irregular verbs correctly.

Irregular Verbs Using *Have, Has,* or *Had:* Past Tense
page 72

1. gone
2. begun
3. grown
4. seen
5. done

Irregular Verbs (1): Past Tense
page 73

1. Earth Week (began yesterday) at our school.
2. We (did) many different activities to celebrate Earth Week.
3. Nina and Leo (went) to a city council meeting to talk about recycling.
4. Some people in the class (ran) in a special Earth Week race.
5. A professor from the college (came) to speak about water pollution yesterday.
6.–10. Sentences will vary but should use the past-tense verb forms *did, began, went, ran,* and *came.*

Irregular Verbs (2): Past Tense
page 74

1. That scientist (gave) a talk to our class about electric cars.
2. The governor (saw) how important protecting the environment is.
3. Weeds (grew) in the vacant lot next to the school.
4. We often (ate) our lunch outside on nice days.
5. The choir (sang) "America the Beautiful."
6.–10. Sentences will vary but should include the past-tense verb forms *saw, grew, gave, sang,* and *ate.*

Irregular Verbs
page 75

Present Tense	Past Tense	Form with *Have, Has,* or *Had*
go	went	gone
come	came	come
begin	began	begun
run	ran	run
do	did	done
eat	ate	eaten
give	gave	given
grow	grew	grown
see	saw	seen
sing	sang	sung

Rachel Carson

Contractions
page 76

Paragraphs should describe the admired person, as well as use contractions correctly.

What Is a Contraction?
page 77

1. couldn't, could not
2. It's, It is
3. isn't, is not
4. won't, will not
5. don't, do not
6. you're, you are
7. can't, cannot
8. I'm, I am
9. hasn't, has not
10. We're, We are

Contractions with a Subject Pronoun and Verb
page 78

1. We're very interested in ponds and lakes.
2. She's a volunteer at the state park.
3. I'm going on a hike this Saturday.
4. It's snowing today.
5. They've collected leaves for a class project.
6. You're coming to the Nature Club meeting.
7. He's taking the newspapers to the recycling center.
8. They're in a big pile in the garage.
9. You've read parts of *Silent Spring* by Rachel Carson.
10. It's important to pick up all the trash.

Contractions with *Not*
page 79

1. Recycling glass and plastic doesn't take a lot of time.
2. Felipe couldn't help clean up the park last week.
3. Some people don't recycle their old newspapers.
4. I wouldn't touch that liquid if I were you.
5. Factories can't dump wastes into the lake.
6. Fish won't live in polluted water.
7. The air here hasn't become polluted.
8. Drivers shouldn't throw papers out of their cars.
9. It isn't smart to litter the playground.
10. My brother and I haven't attended a meeting yet.

Contractions
page 80

Across
1. has not
3. would not
4. will not
5. he is
7. cannot
9. I am
10. you are

Down
2. should not
3. we are
6. she is
8. they are

Unit 5
Pat Cummings: My Story

Pronouns
page 81

Paragraphs should describe and discuss what students like to draw and where they get their ideas, as well as use subject and object pronouns correctly.

What Are Subject and Object Pronouns?
page 82

I, it, He, She, She, I, She, him, It, me

Singular and Plural Subject Pronouns
page 83

Completions will vary.

1. They ride
2. She eats
3. I take
4. It turns
5. He chooses
6. You draw
7. We imagine
8. It says
9. They watch
10. She drinks

Singular and Plural Object Pronouns
page 84

1. We
2. him
3. me
4. her
5. you
6. it
7. us
8. them
9. her
10. They

Using *I* and *me*
page 85

1. a.
2. b.
3. b.
4. b.
5. a.
6. b.
7. b.
8. a.
9. b.
10. b.

The Lucky Stone

Possessive Pronouns
page 86

Paragraphs should describe the favorite item, as well as use possessive pronouns correctly.

What Are Possessive Pronouns?
page 87

1. Have any of you seen (her) lucky rock?
2. That dancing dog (is mine).
3. (His) drawings add a lot to the book.
4. (Their) dresses are wonderful.
5. They were frightened of (its) snarl.
6. Those books (are theirs).
7. Please don't touch (our) display.
8. The book report is (ours).
9. "This is (my) big chance," Richard said to himself.
10. The books on the desk are (hers).

Possessive Pronouns Used Before Nouns
page 88

Answers may vary.

1. your
2. my
3. its
4. their
5. his
6.–10. Sentences will vary.

Possessive Pronouns Used Alone: *mine, yours, his, hers, its, ours, theirs*
page 89

1. hers
2. mine
3. theirs
4. yours
5. his
6. hers
7. mine
8. theirs
9. ours
10. yours

Sentence Combining with Possessive Pronouns
page 90

Sentences may vary.

1. Marcie and Heather turned in their book reports.
2. The red dog and the black and white one are ours.
3. You can both hang your jackets here.
4. The cassette tapes on the desk and on the chair are mine.
5. My sister and I talked to our grandmother on Mother's Day.

Creation of a California Tribe

Adjectives
page 91

Paragraphs should describe the lesson in personal or group history learned, as well as use adjectives correctly.

Adjectives That Tell *What Kind*
page 92

Sentences will vary.

Adjectives That Tell *How Many*
page 93

Answers will vary, but each adjective chosen should make sense in the sentence.

1. (Many) students in our class are interested in history.
2. (One) girl wrote a report on her family history.
3. (Most) students chose to write about our state's history.
4. Our state is one of (fifty) states in the United States.
5. (Two) boys did a project on how Native Americans lived in our state.
6. My report was one of (several) reports on pioneer life.
7. (No) student is more interested in history than I am.
8. There were also (many) projects on our town.

9. (Seven hundred) people lived in this town in the year 1900.
10. (Each) person has his or her own history, too.

A, an, the
page 94

Paragraphs should describe a club from a personal history, as well as use articles correctly.

Adjective After Linking Verbs
page 95

1. underline became, circle interested
2. underline is, circle Mexican American
3. underline were, circle Mexican and Puerto Rican
4. underline is, circle eager
5. underline feels, circle proud
6.–10. Sentences will vary, but each predicate adjective should make sense in the sentence. Students should draw a line linking the predicate adjective and subject.

No Star Nights

Comparative Adjectives
page 96

Paragraphs should compare and contrast the holidays, as well as use comparative and superlative adjectives correctly.

Comparative Adjectives: -er or more
page 97

The following words should be underlined:
1. darker
2. more dangerous
3. larger
4. taller
5. more interested
6.–10. Sentences will vary but must use -er or more to show comparison between the two nouns given.

Superlative Adjectives: -est or most
page 98

1. most delicious
2. sweatiest
3. greatest
4. loudest
5. most fascinating
6. Zahara has the (shortest) walk home from school.
7. The report about coal mining was the (most interesting).
8. C
9. The hot dogs at Forbes Field in Pittsburgh are the (tastiest) I've ever eaten!
10. After West Virginia, Illinois was the (flattest) place I'd ever seen.

Proofing Paragraph with Adjectives that Compare
page 99

To me, the Fourth of July is the (most exciting) holiday of the year. I am probably (busier) at that time than at any other time. I bet I've built (more) floats than anybody I know. Building a float in July can be hot work! That month is probably the (hottest) one in our state. Sometimes we work on the floats at night because it's (cooler) than in the day. It's a fantastic feeling when our float wins first prize in the parade.

Comparative Adjectives
page 100

The following words should be circled:
1. littlest
2. younger
3. high
4. most
5. funnier
6. cutest
7. happier
8. most popular
9. slowest
10. most beautiful

Unit 6
Yeh-Shen

Adverbs That Tell *How*
page 101
Paragraphs should describe the real or desired pet, as well as use adverbs correctly.

What Is an Adverb?
page 102
The adverb is listed first, the verb modified second.

1. curiously; looked
2. happily; ate
3. Quickly; hid
4. softly; sang
5. ell; sews

6. carefully; Listen
7. quickly; ran
8. Silently; walked
9. correctly; copy
10. sadly; returned

Adverbs That Tell *How*
page 103
1. circle beautifully
2. circle lovingly
3. circle proudly
4. circle Quietly
5. circle eagerly

Adverbs will vary. Sample answers are given.

6. Wearily, the man continued his search for the puppy's owner.
7. You will be able to read this book if you plan your time wisely.
8. Work quickly, but be careful.
9. Eagerly, the girl chose the brown puppy.
10. She smiled broadly when she saw its floppy ears.

Placement of Adverbs That Tell *How* in Sentences
page 104
Adverbs will vary. Sample answers are given.

1. If you look closely, you can see drawings of the city.
2. Pick up the injured bird carefully.
3. We ran swiftly to the picnic shelter.
4. The crow screeched loudly when it looked at us.
5. Gracefully, the dancers moved across the stage.
6. Mother sternly reminded him to clean his room.
7. The story ends happily for all the mystery lovers.
8. Secretly, she took the girl's jacket.
9. She cried sadly when she found the coat was torn.
10. The artist draws horses well.

Using *Good* and *Well* Correctly
page 105
1. There are lots of (good) books about China.
2. Stories from other lands match the story of Cinderella quite (well).
3. In each tale, the young girl is kind and (good).
4. But her family does not treat her (well) at all.
5. The girl is a (good) dancer.
6. She dances so (well) at the ball that all eyes are on her.
7. There is usually someone who gives (good) advice.
8. The young girl follows the advice very (well).
9. The stepmother makes a (good) plan.
10. The king or prince always has a (good) disguise.

The Three Little Pigs and the Fox

Adverbs That Tell *Where* and *When*
page 106

Paragraphs should accurately describe the animal, as well as use *where* and *when* adverbs correctly.

Adverbs That Tell *Where*
page 107

Sentences will vary.

Adverbs That Tell *When*
page 108

Sentences will vary.

Placement of Adverbs That Tell *Where* or *When* in Sentences
page 109

Sentences will vary.

Adverbs That Tell *Where* and *When*
page 110

Sentences will vary.

Mufaro's Beautiful Daughters

Adverbs That Compare
page 111

Paragraphs should compare and contrast the family members, as well as use comparative and superlative adverbs correctly.

Adverbs That Compare *How*
page 112

1. *C*
2. One sister acts (more kindly) than the other.
3. She practices (more carefully) than her sister.
4. *C*
5. These crops grew (more quickly) than those over there.
6. Conchita sews (better) than Ramona.
7. I would be a good sewer if I worked (more slowly).
8. We finished our section of the quilt (more easily) than any other group.

Adverbs That Compare *Where*
page 113

(Sentences will vary slightly.)

1. My mom's parents live (closer) to us than my dad's parents.
2. Which airplane flew the (highest)?
3. Move your sleeping bag (nearer) to the campfire.
4. I threw the ball the (farthest) of anyone in the contest.
5. Which cat sleeps (nearer) to the bed, Winky or Mittens?
6. Who can sing the (lowest) in the choir?
7. The red squirrel climbed (higher) in the maple tree than the gray one.
8. Which of your friends lives the (closest) to you?
9. This pitcher throws the ball (lower) than the last pitcher.
10. Lateeka lives (nearest) to me of all my good friends.

Adverbs That Compare *When*
page 114

(Sentences will vary slightly.)

1. The first sister arrived in the city (earlier) than the other.
2. You can come to the meeting (later) if you don't want to hear the speech.
3. I walk to school (more frequently) than I ride my bike.
4. The postcard got here from Africa (sooner) than I expected.
5. Which movie have you seen (most recently): *Jaws, Raiders of the Lost Ark,* or *Batman*?
6. We see our cousins (more often) than most people since they live across the street.
7. What is the (earliest) you can come to the game?
8. Chris handed in her test (latest) of all.
9. Dad watches basketball the (most often) of all sports.
10. Whoever arrives the (earliest) will win the door prize.

Adverbs That Compare
page 115

Sentences will vary.

The Stonecutter

Double Negatives
page 116

Students should write reasonable rules, as well as use negatives correctly.

Common Negatives
page 117

Rewritten sentences may vary.

Cutting stone is no easy job. Nothing is harder than stone to cut, shape, and polish. Nobody can imagine how difficult it can be. In addition, nowhere is a harder place to work than on a mountainside. There is no job that takes more skill than cutting stone.

Common Negative Contractions: *can't, don't, won't*
page 118

1. Camels (don't) need to drink water for long periods of time.
2. The caravan (can't) pass because of the terrible sandstorm.
3. It (won't) be able to leave until tomorrow.
4. We (can't) see with all this sand blowing in the air.
5. I hope tomorrow (won't) be like this in the desert.
6.–10. Sentences will vary.

Common Negative Contractions: *couldn't, doesn't, shouldn't*
page 119

1. People (shouldn't) be unhappy with their work.
2. They (couldn't) do well if they were worried.
3. The merchant (shouldn't) stop for rest and refreshment.
4. The engineer (doesn't) like his work on the mountainside.
5. He (couldn't) be famous.
6. The sun (doesn't) beat down on a foggy day.
7. You (shouldn't) gaze at the sun.
8. Even sunglasses (couldn't) protect your eyes.
9. The wind (doesn't) break up the clouds.
10. The wind (couldn't) be blocked by a mountain.

Double Negatives
page 120

Sentences will vary slightly.

1. Nothing (can) move a mountain.
2. Doesn't (anyone) want to be a stonecutter?
3. The night is so cloudy I can't see (anything).
4. You (will never) be able to ride that camel!
5. Nobody (would help) me polish this block of stone.
6. We (haven't ever) eaten anything so delicious as a sherbet.
7. I would offer you a sherbet, but there (are none) left.
8. No one (could keep) the sun from burning the king's skin.
9. There (is no reason) why he should be so unhappy.
10. The stonecutter (would wear) no shoes but slippers.

WEEKLY ASSESSMENT PARAGRAPHS

The purpose of the weekly assessment paragraphs is to evaluate students' ability to recognize and correct errors in grammar and spelling in a proofreading context.

There are thirty-six paragraphs, divided into six six-week units of work. Each paragraph contains five grammar errors and five spelling errors. The first four weeks of each unit contain errors that correspond to selection-related grammar skills and spelling words. The fifth and sixth weeks of each unit are review weeks and cover grammar skills and spelling words taught in the previous four weeks.

Format of the Paragraphs

The paragraphs are arranged one above the other. At the top is the paragraph to be corrected; below it is the corrected paragraph. In the corrected paragraph, the correctly respelled words are indicated with a double underline; the corrected grammar errors are indicated with a single underline. At the bottom of each page are two scoring boxes, one for spelling and one for grammar.

Using the Paragraphs

You may wish to photocopy the assessment paragraphs for distribution to your students. As an alternative to having students work individually, you may wish to have them complete the work in pairs or small groups, encouraging them to explain to each other why they are making the corrections as they go along.

Spelling Grammar

5   5

Find and fix five spelling errors in the paragraph. Then correct five errors in capitalization and end punctuation of sentences.

We read a folktale from India? Chandra saved the elephants, and the Rajah made a vowe to reward her. A croud gathered inside the palace everyone wanted to see what Chandra would decied to ask for. There was a lowd groan when she asked only for rice to be put on the chessboard. What a strange request She wanted two grains on the first square, four grains on the second square, and so on. Did you think Chandra was smart to understand the pouwer of two.

We read a folktale from India. Chandra saved the elephants, and the Rajah made a <u>vow</u> to reward her. A <u>crowd</u> gathered inside the palace. Everyone wanted to see what Chandra would <u>decide</u> to ask for. There was a <u>loud</u> groan when she asked only for rice to be put on the chessboard. What a strange request! She wanted two grains on the first square, four grains on the second square, and so on. Did you think Chandra was smart to understand the <u>power</u> of two?

Spelling Grammar

5   5

Find and fix five spelling errors in the paragraph. Then add five subjects or predicates to turn fragments into complete sentences.

My dad told me about a time when he and his brother. Had nothing to do and were bored. Decided to make a flying machine. They rigged up a rope on a poolley and attached a large basket to the rope with a huk. My dad was smaller, so he climbed into the basket. Poushed him off the garage roof. Of course, the whole thing fell apart, and my dad fell. My poor dad. It's a good thing some boushes were there to cooshion his fall!

(Sentence answers will vary.)

My dad told me about a time when he and his brother <u>were kids</u>. <u>They</u> had nothing to do and were bored. <u>They</u> decided to make a flying machine. They rigged up a rope on a <u>pulley</u> and attached a large basket to the rope with a <u>hook</u>. My dad was smaller, so he climbed into the basket. <u>My uncle</u> <u>pushed</u> him off the garage roof. Of course, the whole thing fell apart, and my dad fell. My poor dad <u>almost broke his neck.</u> It's a good thing some <u>bushes</u> were there to <u>cushion</u> his fall!

Spelling Grammar

5   5

Find and fix five spelling errors in the paragraph. Then use the simple subjects and predicates printed in italics to form longer complete sentences.

Aunt Jane/called She wanted to take me on a hiking trip. We took sleeping bags, and I carried lunch, my toothpaste, and a coame in my napsack. *Aunt Jane/drove* She wanted to clime to a certain place she remembered. *we/hiked* That night we camped beside a stream high in the mountains. *sun/rose* It was still early morning when we reached the meadow. We saw the dew glissen on the grass. *birds/sang* In the meadow, there were hundreds of blue flowers as high as my nee. It was beautiful—just as Aunt Jane remembered it.

(Sentence answers will vary.)

<u>One day last summer, Aunt Jane called my parents</u>. She wanted to take me on a hiking trip. We took sleeping bags, and I carried lunch, my toothpaste, and a <u>comb</u> in my <u>knapsack</u>. <u>Aunt Jane drove all night</u>. She wanted to <u>climb</u> to a certain place she remembered. <u>We hiked up the mountain all morning and all afternoon</u>. That night we camped beside a stream high in the mountains. <u>We got up as soon as the sun rose the next day</u>. It was still early morning when we reached the meadow. We saw the dew <u>glisten</u> on the grass. <u>Birds sang sweetly everywhere</u>. In the meadow, there were hundreds of blue flowers as high as my <u>knee</u>. It was beautiful—just as Aunt Jane remembered it.

Spelling Grammar

5   5

Find and fix five spelling errors in the paragraphs. Then find five places where sentences can be combined.

We read the story *Sarah, Plain and Tall.* Caleb had groan up so far without a mother. Caleb wanted a mother. Anna wanted a mother. There mother had died when Caleb was born. Papa wrote an advertisement, which Sarah answered. Sarah said she was plane. Sarah said she was tall. She wrote several letters to Papa. She wrote several letters to the children. Then she came for a visit.

Sarah was from Maine and had a reel love for the sea. At first, she was lonely. Maggie came to visit Sarah. Maggie came to give Sarah plants for a flour garden. Sarah still missed the sea. Sarah grew to love the farm.

(Sentence answers may vary.)

We read the story *Sarah, Plain and Tall.* Caleb had <u>grown</u> up so far without a mother. <u>Caleb and Anna wanted a mother</u>. <u>Their</u> mother had died when Caleb was born. Papa wrote an advertisement, which Sarah answered. <u>Sarah said she was plain and tall</u>. <u>She wrote several letters to Papa and the children</u>. Then she came for a visit.

Sarah was from Maine and had a <u>real</u> love for the sea. At first, she was lonely. <u>Maggie came to visit Sarah and to give her plants for a flower garden</u>. <u>Sarah still missed the sea, but she grew to love the farm</u>.

Spelling Grammar

5   5

WEEKLY ASSESSMENT PARAGRAPH
WEEK 5

Find and fix five spelling errors in the paragraph. Then correct three errors in the formation of sentences, and find two places where sentences can be combined.

I wish I could visit my uncle Anton's country house again. His house has ivey growing on it. His house has an evergreen hedje in front. Tall elem trees in his back yard. There is a huge fireplace in the living room. did you ever smell hickry wood burning. We have lunch on the front porch. We drink tea Uncle Anton makes from minte he grows in his garden.

(Sentence answers may vary slightly.)

I wish I could visit my uncle Anton's country house again. <u>His house has ivy growing on it and an evergreen hedge in front</u>. Tall <u>elm</u> trees <u>grow</u> in his back yard. There is a huge fireplace in the living room. <u>Did</u> you ever smell <u>hickory</u> wood burning? <u>We have lunch on the front porch, and we drink tea Uncle Anton makes from mint</u> he grows in his garden.

Spelling Grammar

5   5

Find and fix five spelling errors in the paragraph. Then correct four errors in the formation of sentences, and find one place where two sentences can be combined.

Did you ever want to make ginjer cookies Made some for the first time last week. I stirred sugar, butter, and an egg with a woden spoon. Then I added flower. I added baking powder. next, I added ginger, my favorite spise. I carefully poshed the tray of cookies into the oven and baked them until they were done. Were they ever good?

Did you ever want to make <u>ginger</u> cookies<u>? I</u> made some for the first time last week. I stirred sugar, butter, and an egg with a <u>wooden</u> spoon. <u>Then I added flour and baking powder.</u> <u>N</u>ext, I added ginger, my favorite <u>spice</u>. I carefully <u>pushed</u> the tray of cookies into the oven and baked them until they were done. Were they ever good<u>!</u>

Spelling Grammar

5 5

WEEKLY ASSESSMENT PARAGRAPH
WEEK 7

Find and fix five spelling errors in the paragraph. Then correct five errors in the use of proper and common nouns.

The inuit people of alaska and Canada depended on plants and animals of the Arctic to survive. In winter, they would hunt Seals and whales from the jaged ice floes in the arctic ocean. The bluber from these animals helped give them energy. They might find a riben of open water and hunt from a kayak. In summer, they would hunt caribou or find berries and an occasional bird's egge. In june and July they could hunt all night, because in the midel of summer, the sun never sets in the Arctic.

The <u>Inuit</u> people of <u>Alaska</u> and Canada depended on plants and animals of the Arctic to survive. In winter, they would hunt <u>seals</u> and whales from the <u>jagged</u> ice floes in the <u>Arctic Ocean</u>. The <u>blubber</u> from these animals helped give them energy. They might find a <u>ribbon</u> of open water and hunt from a kayak. In summer, they would hunt caribou or find berries and an occasional bird's <u>egg</u>. In <u>June</u> and July they could hunt all night, because in the <u>middle</u> of summer, the sun never sets in the Arctic.

Spelling Grammar

5   5

Find and fix five spelling errors in the paragraphs. Then correct five errors in the formation of plural nouns.

On our vacashin last summer, we stayed at a tourest cabin in the mountaines. One day we saw a black bear and her cubs eating berrys. One queston I've always had about bears is, how do they sleep through the winter?

In addishin, we saw two baby foxs playing in a meadow. We watched them for a while through field glasss. We also saw a flock of wild turkies one morning. I get a lot of enjoymint from watching wildlife.

On our <u>vacation</u> last summer, we stayed at a <u>tourist</u> cabin in the <u>mountains</u>. One day we saw a black bear and her cubs eating <u>berries</u>. One <u>question</u> I've always had about bears is, how do they sleep through the winter?

In <u>addition</u>, we saw two baby <u>foxes</u> playing in a meadow. We watched them for a while through field <u>glasses</u>. We also saw a flock of wild <u>turkeys</u> one morning. I get a lot of <u>enjoyment</u> from watching wildlife.

Spelling Grammar

5   5

Find and fix five spelling errors in the paragraphs. Then correct five errors in the formation of plural nouns.

What do animals do in winter? Many, but not all, birds avoyd bad weather by flying south. In some places gooses stay the winter because peoples feed them. Toads use their strong back feets to dig themselves a hole below the frost line. Frogs hibernate under the mud in ponds until warm weather returns. If you live near a pond, you might hear the voace of a bullfrog in spring or a noysie chorus of spring peepers.

Many mammals stay active all winter. Field mouses store seeds, but are active at night through tunnels in the snow. In summer, deers have a choyce of leaves and other things to eat, but in winter food is scarce. They often annoiy homeowners by eating the shrubs around houses.

What do animals do in winter? Many, but not all, birds <u>avoid</u> bad weather by flying south. In some places <u>geese</u> stay the winter because <u>people</u> feed them. Toads use their strong back <u>feet</u> to dig themselves a hole below the frost line. Frogs hibernate under the mud in ponds until warm weather returns. If you live near a pond, you might hear the <u>voice</u> of a bullfrog in spring or a <u>noisy</u> chorus of spring peepers.

Many mammals stay active all winter. Field <u>mice</u> store seeds, but are active at night through tunnels in the snow. In summer, <u>deer</u> have a <u>choice</u> of leaves and other things to eat, but in winter food is scarce. They often <u>annoy</u> homeowners by eating the shrubs around houses.

Spelling Grammar

5   5

WEEKLY ASSESSMENT PARAGRAPH
WEEK 10

Find and fix five spelling errors in the paragraph. Then correct five errors in the formation of possessive nouns.

Animals homes may be found almost anywhere. A crak in the pavement might hide an ants nest. A sawarm of bees may make their hive in a hollow tree. Some kinds of fish swim together in groops called schools, but they have no real home. They may lay their eggs in the geravel at the bottom of a stream. A mouses winter home may be reached through a tunnel in the snoe. A squirrels nest is found high in a tree. Beavers lodges are usually built in the middle of ponds.

Animals' homes may be found almost anywhere. A crack in the pavement might hide an ants' nest. A swarm of bees may make their hive in a hollow tree. Some kinds of fish swim together in groups called schools, but they have no real home. They may lay their eggs in the gravel at the bottom of a stream. A mouse's winter home may be reached through a tunnel in the snow. A squirrel's nest is found high in a tree. Beavers' lodges are usually built in the middle of ponds.

Spelling	Grammar
5	5

Find and fix five spelling errors in the paragraph. Then correct five errors in the formation of proper, possessive, and plural nouns.

My kittey, pumpkin, thinks he is a great hunter. One night he chased a mawth around the living room. He jumped on my mothers desk and scattered some important papers. Sometimes he tries to catch the bird inside the kookoo clock. I think he does it just for a lawrk. Still another time he waited in the bushs near the barn. He was just about to pounce on two mouses when a big hawke swooped down to grab them. Pumpkin let out a loud screech. The mice escaped. My brave hunter saved the mices lives!

My <u>kitty</u>, <u>Pumpkin</u>, thinks he is a great hunter. One night he chased a <u>moth</u> around the living room. He jumped on my <u>mother's</u> desk and scattered some important papers. Sometimes he tries to catch the bird inside the <u>cuckoo</u> clock. I think he does it just for a <u>lark</u>. Still another time he waited in the <u>bushes</u> near the barn. He was just about to pounce on two <u>mice</u> when a big <u>hawk</u> swooped down to grab them. Pumpkin let out a loud screech. The mice escaped. My brave hunter saved the <u>mice's</u> lives!

Spelling	Grammar
5	5

Find and fix five spelling errors in the paragraph. Then correct five errors in the formation of proper, possessive, and plural nouns.

One of my cousin Tonys hobbeys is to photograph wildlife. He sometimes climbs grandfather mountain in north carolina. Tony once lay on the jaggid rocks near the top of the mountain to take a photo of a hauk. He took another picture of two deers in the snow. These beautiful photos are now hanging in my aunts apartmint. Tony is really an artest with a camera.

One of my cousin <u>Tony's</u> <u>hobbies</u> is to photograph wildlife. He sometimes climbs <u>Grandfather Mountain</u> in <u>North Carolina</u>. Tony once lay on the <u>jagged</u> rocks near the top of the mountain to take a photo of a <u>hawk</u>. He took another picture of two <u>deer</u> in the snow. These beautiful photos are now hanging in my <u>aunt's</u> <u>apartment</u>. Tony is really an <u>artist</u> with a camera.

Spelling Grammar

5   5

Find and fix five spelling errors in the paragraph. Then underline five action verbs.

Before her marridge to my uncle, my aunt worked in an office. Her hart was not in it. Then one day in the liberry, she saw an advertisement for a job at The Seeing Eye. This school trains gide dogs for the blind. My aunt has turned her intrest in animals into a job that she loves.

Before her <u>marriage</u> to my uncle, my aunt <u>worked</u> in an office. Her <u>heart</u> was not in it. Then one day in the <u>library</u>, she <u>saw</u> an advertisement for a job at The Seeing Eye. This school <u>trains</u> <u>guide</u> dogs for the blind. My aunt has <u>turned</u> her <u>interest</u> in animals into a job that she <u>loves</u>.

Spelling Grammar

5   5

Find and fix five spelling errors in the paragraphs. Then correct five errors in the formation of present-tense verbs.

Doring my summer vacation, I sometimes visits my uncle and aunt. Amung the things my uncle can do well is bake. He bake the best apple pies. He has promised to teach me to make pie cruss the way he does.

My uncle and aunt both ride mountain bicycles, too. They rides every shance they get. They often travels a great distanse to go to a rally. My aunt sometimes win prizes for her riding skill.

During my summer vacation, I sometimes visit my uncle and aunt. Among the things my uncle can do well is bake. He bakes the best apple pies. He has promised to teach me to make pie crust the way he does.

My uncle and aunt both ride mountain bicycles, too. They ride every chance they get. They often travel a great distance to go to a rally. My aunt sometimes wins prizes for her riding skill.

Spelling	Grammar
/5	/5

Find and fix five spelling errors in the paragraph. Then correct five errors in the formation of past-tense verbs.

In Octobre my class putted on a play. Last week they decide to do another one in decembre, for Chrissmas. Yesterday some of the kids tryed out for it. My best friend Toni and I stay after school and watched. When John steped onstage to sing, everyone applauded. I hope to try out for the next play. It will be in Januery or Febuary.

In <u>October</u> my class <u>put</u> on a play. Last week they <u>decided</u> to do another one in <u>December</u>, for <u>Christmas</u>. Yesterday some of the kids <u>tried</u> out for it. My best friend Toni and I <u>stayed</u> after school and watched. When John <u>stepped</u> onstage to sing, everyone applauded. I hope to try out for the next play. It will be in <u>January</u> or <u>February</u>.

Spelling Grammar

5   5

WEEKLY ASSESSMENT PARAGRAPHS
WEEK 16

Find and fix five spelling errors in the paragraphs. Then correct five errors in the use of *be, have,* or *do*.

In the 1930s and 1940s, many public places in the United States was segregated. A black person could not use the same batroom or drinking fountain as a white person. Many buses and rail-road cars was segregated, too. Many hotels and restaurants would not serve blacks. Some people thought that this was alright, but other people thought it was unfair.

Major league baseball were segregated, too. Branch Rickey wanted to change this. He done something very important for baseball by hiring Jackie Robinson. He knew Robinson was a special person, with great talents and personal qualities.

Robinson played first-base for the Brooklyn Dodgers. Pee Wee Reese, his teamate, also proved he have great courage.

In the 1930s and 1940s, many public places in the United States <u>were</u> segregated. A black person could not use the same <u>bathroom</u> or drinking fountain as a white person. Many buses and <u>railroad</u> cars <u>were</u> segregated, too. Many hotels and restaurants would not serve blacks. Some people thought that this was <u>all right</u>, but other people thought it was unfair.

Major league baseball <u>was</u> segregated, too. Branch Rickey wanted to change this. He <u>did</u> something very important for baseball by hiring Jackie Robinson. He knew Robinson was a special person, with great talents and personal qualities.

Robinson played <u>first base</u> for the Brooklyn Dodgers. Pee Wee Reese, his <u>teammate</u>, also proved he <u>had</u> great courage.

Spelling	Grammar
5	5

Find and fix five spelling errors in the paragraph. Then correct three errors in the use of *be, have,* or *do* and two errors in the formation of present-tense or past-tense verbs.

My friend Mandy and I has always liked different kinds of food. Last night Mandy's dad cook a spicey Cajun dish. Mandy said it was too hot, but I thought it was very tastey. One of my favorite meals are chicken with crunchie snow peas. I likes the sweet taste of peas, but Mandy do not. She prefers saltie foods. I think she would even eat stail potato chips.

My friend Mandy and I <u>have</u> always liked different kinds of food. Last night Mandy's dad <u>cooked</u> a <u>spicy</u> Cajun dish. Mandy said it was too hot, but I thought it was very <u>tasty</u>. One of my favorite meals <u>is</u> chicken with <u>crunchy</u> snow peas. I <u>like</u> the sweet taste of peas, but Mandy <u>does</u> not. She prefers <u>salty</u> foods. I think she would even eat <u>stale</u> potato chips.

Spelling Grammar

5   5

Find and fix five spelling errors in the paragraph. Then correct three errors in the use of *be, have,* or *do* and two errors in the formation of present-tense or past-tense verbs.

Last summer my friend Joey and I was on the same baseball team. In Awgust we playd a game agenst our rivals, the Panthers. Joey and Bobbie, another teemmate, was the only ones to get any hits. I is not much of a hitter, but I make a good catch that kept a run from scoring. It made a diffrence, because we won by one run. I still gots the story that the newespaper printed about that game.

Last summer my friend Joey and I <u>were</u> on the same baseball team. In <u>August</u> we <u>played</u> a game <u>against</u> our rivals, the Panthers. Joey and Bobbie, another <u>teammate</u>, were the only ones to get any hits. I <u>am</u> not much of a hitter, but I <u>made</u> a good catch that kept a run from scoring. It made a <u>difference</u>, because we won by one run. I still <u>have</u> the story that the <u>newspaper</u> printed about that game.

Spelling	Grammar
/ 5	/ 5

Find and fix five spelling errors in the paragraph. Then correct five errors in the use of helping verbs.

There is only one place to play sports in my town, and the high school teams practice there all the time. But now something changed. Mom and I was driving past a vacant feeld last week. It was full of peeple who are clearing the brush. We found out that a man have given monie so the town could buy this peace of property for a park. Now it are becoming a place where kids can play voleyball and hockie.

There is only one place to play sports in my town, and the high school teams practice there all the time. But now something <u>has</u> changed. Mom and I <u>were</u> driving past a vacant <u>field</u> last week. It was full of people who <u>were</u> clearing the brush. We found out that a man <u>had</u> given <u>money</u> so the town could buy this <u>piece</u> of property for a park. Now it <u>is</u> becoming a place where kids can play <u>volleyball</u> and <u>hockey</u>.

Spelling	Grammar
5	5

Find and fix five spelling errors in the paragraphs. Then correct five errors in the use of linking verbs.

Whales is very interesting animals. A killer whale, or orca, are one kind of whale. An orca travels and feeds in a hurd called a pod. The gray whale feeds in an unusual way. It blows watir out of its mouth to stur up sand on the ocean bottom. Then it sucks in the sediment and feeds.

Judy Collins are a folk singer. She once recorded a song that used the sounds of humpback whales in the background. These whale songs is very beautiful. I hope we can presurve the whales. They was once numerous in every ocean. I would like to see the retorn of those large whale populations.

Whales <u>are</u> very interesting animals. A killer whale, or orca, <u>is</u> one kind of whale. An orca travels and feeds in a <u>herd</u> called a pod. The gray whale feeds in an unusual way. It blows <u>water</u> out of its mouth to <u>stir</u> up sand on the ocean bottom. Then it sucks in the sediment and feeds.

Judy Collins <u>is</u> a folk singer. She once recorded a song that used the sounds of humpback whales in the background. These whale songs <u>are</u> very beautiful. I hope we can <u>preserve</u> the whales. They <u>were</u> once numerous in every ocean. I would like to see the <u>return</u> of those large whale populations.

Spelling	Grammar
5	5

Find and fix five spelling errors in the paragraph. Then correct five errors in the formation of irregular verbs.

The principle of our school talked to us last week. He has did that before. He knowed our teachers teached us about pollution and recycling. He telled us that pollution is a nationel problem. He said it is possibel for us to affect the future. He said there are no simpel answers to some problems, but he gived us a challenge. He asked us if we would take the troubel to help set up a recycling center in our town.

The <u>principal</u> of our school talked to us last week. He has <u>done</u> that before. He <u>knew</u> our teachers <u>taught</u> us about pollution and recycling. He <u>told</u> us that pollution is a <u>national</u> problem. He said it is <u>possible</u> for us to affect the future. He said there are no <u>simple</u> answers to some problems, but he <u>gave</u> us a challenge. He asked us if we would take the <u>trouble</u> to help set up a recycling center in our town.

Spelling Grammar

5   5

Find and fix five spelling errors in the paragraph. Then correct five errors in the formation of contractions.

My friend invented a computer game. It isnt the usual kind of game. He didnt want to make just another game about fighting a dragen or rescuing someone from a dunjin. Instead, its about the danger of using pesticides. Pesticides are poisons, so of course they arent any more healthy for a humen than for a bug. In my friend's game, a player who cant defeat the chemical demin turns into a skeletun at the end.

My friend invented a computer game. It <u>isn't</u> the usual kind of game. He <u>didn't</u> want to make just another game about fighting a <u>dragon</u> or rescuing someone from a <u>dungeon</u>. Instead, <u>it's</u> about the danger of using pesticides. Pesticides are poisons, so of course they <u>aren't</u> any more healthy for a <u>human</u> than for a bug. In my friend's game, a player who <u>can't</u> defeat the chemical <u>demon</u> turns into a <u>skeleton</u> at the end.

Spelling Grammar

5 5

Find and fix five spelling errors in the paragraph. Then correct four errors in the use of helping, linking, or irregular verbs and one error in the formation of a contraction.

My mother brung home my beagle puppy, Bungle, when he is six weeks old. He liked to slinke along the kitchen floor on his belly. Now that he are older, he has become a nature lover. He likes to meandre through the field near my house. He been known to stawlk butterflies, but he never catches any. Im not afraid he will waonder too far, though. He always seems to marche back just in time for supper.

My mother _brought_ home my beagle puppy, Bungle, when he _was_ six weeks old. He liked to _slink_ along the kitchen floor on his belly. Now that he _is_ older, he has become a nature lover. He likes to _meander_ through the field near my house. He _has been_ known to _stalk_ butterflies, but he never catches any. _I'm_ not afraid he will _wander_ too far, though. He always seems to _march_ back just in time for supper.

Spelling	Grammar
5	5

Find and fix five spelling errors in the paragraphs. Then correct three errors in the use of helping, linking, or irregular verbs and two errors in the formation of contractions.

When I was eight, I goed to the hospitle to have my appendix out. After the operation, the nurse told me to stay in bed and not to stur. I was pretty lonely, because both my parents was working. All the doctors and nurses tried to cheer me up. Still, I could hardly wait to retuorn home. Then my uncle comed to visit me.

"Howse my favorite neice?" he bellowed.

I didnt think it was possabel, but soon he was telling me jokes and making me smile.

When I was eight, I <u>went</u> to the <u>hospital</u> to have my appendix out. After the operation, the nurse told me to stay in bed and not to <u>stir</u>. I was pretty lonely, because both my parents <u>were</u> working. All the doctors and nurses tried to cheer me up. Still, I could hardly wait to <u>return</u> home. Then my uncle <u>came</u> to visit me.

"<u>How's</u> my favorite <u>niece</u>?" he bellowed.

I <u>didn't</u> think it was <u>possible</u>, but soon he was telling me jokes and making me smile.

Spelling Grammar

5   5

Find and fix five spelling errors in the paragraphs. Then correct five errors in the use of pronouns.

Pat Cummings always wanted to be an artist. She never thought of being a docter or a farmer. Her wanted to illustrate children's books. Finally, an editer asked she to do the pictures for a book. She called up Tom Feelings, another artist. He did her a big faver by helping she get started.

My favorite children's book authur and illustrator is Chris Van Allsburg. I liked the way him used colir in *Just a Dream.* Cummings, Feelings, and Van Allsburg are all lucky. Them get paid to draw and paint.

Pat Cummings always wanted to be an artist. She never thought of being a <u>doctor</u> or a farmer. <u>She</u> wanted to illustrate children's books. Finally, an <u>editor</u> asked <u>her</u> to do the pictures for a book. She called up Tom Feelings, another artist. He did her a big <u>favor</u> by helping <u>her</u> get started.

My favorite children's book <u>author</u> and illustrator is Chris Van Allsburg. I liked the way <u>he</u> used <u>color</u> in *Just a Dream.* Cummings, Feelings, and Van Allsburg are all lucky. <u>They</u> get paid to draw and paint.

Spelling	Grammar
5	5

Find and fix five spelling errors in the paragraphs. Then correct five errors in the use of possessive nouns.

My grandmother told me that she and hir sister once went to a street fair. They both threw balls to try and win a teddy bear. Each girl wanted it to be her's. After the twelvth try, they had a quarel. My grandmother's sister wanted to qwit, but my grandmother stayed to watch as a qwiet young man took his's turn. He threw twise and won!

"It's your's," he said, as he gave the teddy bear to my grandmother.

Someday, Grandma promised, the teddy bear Grandpa won for her would be mines.

My grandmother told me that she and <u>her</u> sister once went to a street fair. They both threw balls to try and win a teddy bear. Each girl wanted it to be <u>hers</u>. After the <u>twelfth</u> try, they had a <u>quarrel</u>. My grandmother's sister wanted to <u>quit</u>, but my grandmother stayed to watch as a <u>quiet</u> young man took <u>his</u> turn. He threw <u>twice</u> and won!

"It's <u>yours</u>," he said, as he gave the teddy bear to my grandmother.

Someday, Grandma promised, the teddy bear Grandpa won for her would be <u>mine</u>.

Spelling Grammar

5   5

Find and fix five spelling errors in the paragraph. Then fill in the blanks with two adjectives and three article-and-adjective combinations.

     There are many trible stories about the creaytion of the world. _____ tales give _____ explanashun of how the world came to be. I found reading these tales very enjoyible. We read _____ tale from the Maidu people of California. _____ characters in _____ tale are Earth Maker and Coyote. They worked together to creeayte the world and its people and animals.

(Adjective answers will vary.)

     There are many <u>tribal</u> stories about the <u>creation</u> of the world. <u>The old</u> tales give <u>an unusual</u> <u>explanation</u> of how the world came to be. I found reading these tales very <u>enjoyable</u>. We read <u>one</u> tale from the Maidu people of California. <u>The main</u> characters in <u>this</u> tale are Earth Maker and Coyote. They worked together to <u>create</u> the world and its people and animals.

Spelling Grammar

5   5

WEEKLY ASSESSMENT PARAGRAPHS
WEEK 28

Find and fix five spelling errors in the paragraphs. Then correct five errors in the formation of adjectives that compare.

Grandpa tells me that when he was growing up on a dairy farm, the summers were the funnest. He picked berryes along the creek and ate the juicyest tomatos fresh from the garden. His father always gave him the promisingest of the newborn calfes to raise for the county fair.

When the leafes began to change color, the family knew winter was coming. Grandpa says the winters were cold then than now. There were no oil furnacess to heat the houses, so he and his brothers had to chop firewood—the most hardest chore of all.

Grandpa tells me that when he was growing up on a dairy farm, the summers were the <u>most fun</u>. He picked <u>berries</u> along the creek and ate the <u>juiciest</u> <u>tomatoes</u> fresh from the garden. His father always gave him the <u>most promising</u> of the newborn <u>calves</u> to raise for the county fair.

When the <u>leaves</u> began to change color, the family knew winter was coming. Grandpa says the winters were <u>colder</u> then than now. There were no oil <u>furnaces</u> to heat the houses, so he and his brothers had to chop firewood—the <u>hardest</u> chore of all.

Spelling Grammar
5   5

Find and fix five spelling errors in the paragraph. Then correct three errors in the use of pronouns and two errors in the use of adjectives (including articles).

I helped Nana make a memory quilt. Us used a piece of cordoroy from my dad's pants. We cut a piece of denem from a old pair of blue jeans (they were mines, of course). We used a patch from my sister's saten dress. Won't her be surprised when she sees it? We even used some red plaid flanel from Grandpa's bathrobe. Then we sewed a frinje around the whole quilt. I think it is the beautifullest quilt in the world!

I helped Nana make a memory quilt. <u>We</u> used a piece of <u>corduroy</u> from my dad's pants. We cut a piece of <u>denim</u> from <u>an</u> old pair of blue jeans (they were <u>mine</u>, of course). We used a patch from my sister's <u>satin</u> dress. Won't <u>she</u> be surprised when she sees it? We even used some red plaid <u>flannel</u> from Grandpa's bathrobe. Then we sewed a <u>fringe</u> around the whole quilt. I think it is the <u>most beautiful</u> quilt in the world!

Spelling Grammar

| 5 | 5 |

Find and fix five spelling errors in the paragraph. Then correct three errors in the use of pronouns and two errors in the use of adjectives (including articles).

I decided to write a creashun story of mine own. In my story, a carpentor wanted to build a new world. He used a mirrer for the sky and built hes world inside a great bowl. Him made himself king. Everything was going fine until an terribul storm blew up. The winds were the destructivest ever. Soon the carpenter's world was a complete wreck. I will show my story to the editur of our school paper.

I decided to write a <u>creation</u> story of <u>my</u> own. In my story, a <u>carpenter</u> wanted to build a new world. He used a <u>mirror</u> for the sky and built <u>his</u> world inside a great bowl. <u>He</u> made himself king. Everything was going fine until <u>a</u> <u>terrible</u> storm blew up. The winds were the <u>most destructive</u> ever. Soon the carpenter's world was a complete wreck. I will show my story to the <u>editor</u> of our school paper.

Spelling Grammar

5   5

Find and fix five spelling errors in the paragraph. Then correct five errors in the use of adverbs that tell *how*.

We listened close as our teacher quiet read us a story. We knew immediately that it wasnt *Cinderella* but *Yeh-Shen,* the Chinese tale. Ed Young is the artist who illustrated *Yeh-Shen* so beautiful. Heed also done *Lon Po Po,* which weave read, too. Hes one of my favorite illustrators. When my aunt and uncle gave me a copy of *The Girl Who Loved the Wind* by Jane Yolen, which Young also illustrated, I read it eager. Theyd found it unexpected in an old bookstore.

We listened <u>closely</u> as our teacher <u>quietly</u> read us a story. We knew immediately that it <u>wasn't</u> *Cinderella,* but *Yeh-Shen,* the Chinese tale. Ed Young is the artist who illustrated *Yeh-Shen* so <u>beautifully</u>. <u>He'd</u> also done *Lon Po Po,* which <u>we've</u> read, too. <u>He's</u> one of my favorite illustrators. When my aunt and uncle gave me a copy of *The Girl Who Loved the Wind* by Jane Yolen, which Young also illustrated, I read it <u>eagerly</u>. <u>They'd</u> found it <u>unexpectedly</u> in an old bookstore.

Spelling	Grammar
5	5

Find and fix five spelling errors in the paragraph. Then fill in each blank with an adverb that tells *where* or *when*.

Have you read *The True Story of the Three Little Pigs* by Jon Sciezka? In this version of the tale, the wolf claims he was framed. He wasn't sneeking up on the pigs, or hideing _____ *(where?)* their houses. He was only planning to borrow some sugar, but the pigs wouldn't let him in. They told him to go _____ *(where?).* _____ *(When?),* he just happened to sneeze and blow the houses down. He found the fresh hams just lieing _____ *(where?),* he says. That wolf isn't foolling anyone. He _____ *(when?)* could be trusted. I know he is fibing!

(Adverb answers will vary.)

Have you read *The True Story of the Three Little Pigs* by Jon Sciezka? In this version of the tale, the wolf claims he was framed. He wasn't <u>sneaking</u> up on the pigs, or <u>hiding</u> <u>outside</u> their houses. He was only planning to borrow some sugar, but the pigs wouldn't let him in. They told him to go <u>away</u>. <u>Next</u>, he just happened to sneeze and blow the houses down. He found the fresh hams just <u>lying</u> <u>there</u>, he says. That wolf isn't <u>fooling</u> anyone. He <u>never</u> could be trusted. I know he is <u>fibbing</u>!

Spelling	Grammar
5	5

Find and fix five spelling errors in the paragraphs. Then correct five errors in the use of adverbs that compare.

My class acted out *Mufaro's Beautiful Daughters* as a play. My job was to rite the cene in which Mufaro speaks about raiseing his daughters to be worthy. I worked hardest on that play than on anything else I've ever written. Nyasha treated people more kind than her sister did. She behaved more generous toward everyone. At the end, we knew the king had chosen the wright woman to be his queen. We expected people to be happy with her raign.

Earlyer this year we read *Yeh-Shen,* a Chinese Cinderella story. There are many versions of this old tale. Our teacher promised she would read another one to us sooner.

My class acted out *Mufaro's Beautiful Daughters* as a play. My job was to <u>write</u> the <u>scene</u> in which Mufaro speaks about <u>raising</u> his daughters to be worthy. I worked <u>harder</u> on that play than on anything else I've ever written. Nyasha treated people <u>more kindly</u> than her sister did. She behaved <u>more generously</u> toward everyone. At the end, we knew the king had chosen the <u>right</u> woman to be his queen. We expected people to be happy with her <u>reign</u>.

<u>Earlier</u> this year we read *Yeh-Shen,* a Chinese Cinderella story. There are many versions of this old tale. Our teacher promised she would read another one to us <u>soon</u>.

Spelling	Grammar
5	5

Find and fix five spelling errors in the paragraphs. Then correct five double negatives.

   Once there was a fisherman who never had no luck until he caught a magic fish. He made the fish prommise to grant his wish. The fish agreed, and the fisherman asked for a nice little cottage. But his beuteful dawhter wasn't happy with no cottage. She made her father return and ask for welth. There wasn't no way she'd be content with just riches, either. She made him return again and ask to become a king.

   The fisherman didn't want to do no such thing. But he went back, knowin the fish would be angry. Sure enough, the fish yelled, "Won't you never be satisfied?" Then the fish took away everything, leaving the fisherman poor again.

   Once there was a fisherman who never had <u>any</u> luck until he caught a magic fish. He made the fish <u>promise</u> to grant his wish. The fish agreed, and the fisherman asked for a nice little cottage. But his <u>beautiful</u> <u>daughter</u> wasn't happy with <u>a</u> cottage. She made her father return and ask for <u>wealth</u>. There <u>was</u> no way she'd be content with just riches, either. She made him return again and ask to become a king.

   The fisherman didn't want to do <u>any</u> such thing. But he went back, <u>knowing</u> the fish would be angry. Sure enough, the fish yelled, "Won't you <u>ever</u> be satisfied?" Then the fish took away everything, leaving the fisherman poor again.

Spelling Grammar

| 5 | 5 |

Find and fix five spelling errors in the paragraph. Then correct three errors in the use of adverbs and two double negatives.

One stormey night, my father told my brother and me a scary story. I don't like to hear no spooky tales unless the wind is calme, but my brother and I listened close. Dad told us how a ship had sailed into port on a humed, foggie night. The ship's bell clanged loud. When the townspeople went to investigate, there wasn't nobody on board. Just then, there was a loud clap of thunder, and a cloudberst began. I don't know who jumped highest, my brother or me!

One <u>stormy</u> night, my father told my brother and me a scary story. I don't like to hear <u>any</u> spooky tales unless the wind is <u>calm</u>, but my brother and I listened <u>closely</u>. Dad told us how a ship had sailed into port on a <u>humid</u>, <u>foggy</u> night. The ship's bell clanged <u>loudly</u>. When the townspeople went to investigate, there wasn't <u>anybody</u> on board. Just then, there was a loud clap of thunder, and a <u>cloudburst</u> began. I don't know who jumped <u>higher</u>, my brother or me!

Spelling   Grammar

5   5

Find and fix five spelling errors in the paragraph. Then correct three errors in the use of adverbs and two double negatives.

I told my sister an old tale to try to teach her a lesson. One carackter in the tale was a girl who didn't have no manners, just like my sister. She likes to intarupt people. I have spoken frequent to her about this, but she doesn't never listen to what I say. I dont know what else I can do. She acts rudely than anyone else I know. She's always squerming in her chair, too. I'm not sure whose worse, my sister or our new puppy. My sister certainly yelps more louder. Oh, well, maybe when she is two she will behave better.

I told my sister an old tale to try to teach her a lesson. One <u>character</u> in the tale was a girl who didn't have <u>any</u> manners, just like my sister. She likes to <u>interrupt</u> people. I have spoken <u>frequently</u> to her about this, but she doesn't <u>ever</u> listen to what I say. I <u>don't</u> know what else I can do. She acts <u>more rudely</u> than anyone else I know. She's always <u>squirming</u> in her chair, too. I'm not sure <u>who's</u> worse, my sister or our new puppy. My sister certainly yelps <u>more loudly</u>. Oh, well, maybe when she is two she will behave better.

Spelling	Grammar
5	5